A LIFE OF
Obedience
Andrew Murray

BOOKS BY ANDREW MURRAY

Abiding in Christ
Absolute Surrender
The Believer's School of Prayer
The Blood of Christ
Divine Healing
Humility
Living a Prayerful Life
The Ministry of Intercessory Prayer
The Path to Holiness
The Spirit of Christ
Teach Me to Pray
Waiting on God

A LIFE OF

Obedience

Andrew Murray

BETHANYHOUSE
Minneapolis, Minnesota

A Life of Obedience
Andrew Murray

Copyright © 1982, 2004
Bethany House Publishers

Originally titled *The School of Obedience,* the book was updated in 1982
under the title *The Believer's Secret of Obedience.*
The 2004 edition is newly revised and updated.

Cover design by Eric Walljasper

Scripture quotations are from the New King James Version of the Bible.
Copyright © 1979, 1980, 1982 by Thomas Nelson, Inc., Publishers. Used
by permission. All rights reserved.

Published by Bethany House Publishers
11400 Hampshire Avenue South
Bloomington, Minnesota 55438
www.bethanyhouse.com

Bethany House Publishers is a Division of
Baker Book House Company, Grand Rapids, Michigan.

Printed in the United States of America

Library of Congress Cataloging-in-Publication Data
Murray, Andrew, 1828-1917
   A life of obedience / by Andrew Murray.   p. cm.
Rev. ed. of: The believer's of secret of obedience.
   ISBN 0-7642-2867-6 (pbk.)
   1. Obedience—Religious aspects—Christianity. I. Murray, Andrew.
Believer's secret of obedience. II. Title.   BV4647.02M87 2004
   234'.6—dc22   2003023500

ANDREW MURRAY was born in South Africa in 1828. After receiving his education in Scotland and Holland, he returned to South Africa, where he spent many years as a missionary pastor. He was a staunch advocate of biblical Christianity and is best known for his many devotional books. He and his wife, Emma, raised eight children.

Contents

Chapter 1

The Place of Obedience in Scripture

In a Bible word study or a study of a particular truth of the Christian life, it always helps to examine the place it takes in Scripture or the context of the word. As we see where it is used, how often it is used, and in what connection it is found, its relative importance may be understood as well as its relevance to the whole revelation of Scripture. To prepare the way for the study of "obedience" in Scripture, we need to go to God's Word to find the mind of God.

First, we must take Scripture as a whole. Let us begin with Paradise, which in the beginning was the Garden of Eden. It also refers to where the saints will dwell forever with God in eternity. In Genesis 2:16 we read, "And the LORD God commanded the man . . ." And later (3:11), "Have you eaten from the tree of which I commanded you that you should not eat?" Note how obedience to the command is the one virtue of Paradise, the one condition of man's abiding there, the one thing his Creator asks of him. Nothing is said of faith or humility or love—obedience covers all. Equally as supreme as the claim and authority of God is the demand for obedience—the one thing that decides man's destiny. To obey is the one thing required.

Turn now from the beginning of the Bible to the end. In the last chapter we read (Revelation 22:14), "Blessed are those who do His commandments, that they may have the right to the tree of life." From beginning to end, from Paradise lost to Paradise regained, the law is unchanged: it is obedience that gives access to the tree of life and the favor of God.

How was the change effected? The Cross of Christ. From disobedience at the beginning that closed the way to the tree of life, to obedience at the end that gained entrance to it again, that which stands midway between the beginning and the end is the Cross of Christ. Romans 5:19 says, "For as by one man's disobedience many were made sinners, so also by one Man's obedience many will be made righteous." And Philippians 2:8–9, "And being found in appearance as a man, He humbled Himself and became obedient to the point of death, even the death of the cross. Therefore God also has highly exalted Him." See also Hebrews 5:8–9: "Though He was a Son, yet He learned obedience by the things which He suffered. And having been perfected, He became the author of eternal salvation to all who obey Him." In these verses we can see how the whole redemption of Christ consists in restoring obedience to its place. The beauty of His salvation consists of this, that He brings us back to the life of obedience, through *which alone the creature can give the Creator the glory due to Him, or receive the glory of which his Creator desires him to partake.* Paradise, Calvary, heaven, all proclaim with one voice: Child of God, the first and the last thing your God asks of you is simple, universal, unchanging obedience.

Let us turn to the Old Testament. Especially notice how, with any new beginning in the history of God's kingdom, obedience always comes into special prominence. As to Noah, who became the new father of the human race, we find four times written (Genesis 6:22; 7:5, 9, 16), in effect, "Thus Noah did; according to all that God commanded him, so he did." It is the one who does what God commands to whom God can entrust His work, whom God can use to be a type of savior to others.

Think of Abraham, the father of the chosen race. "By faith Abraham *obeyed*" (Hebrews 11:8). When he had been forty years in this school of faith-obedience, God came to perfect his faith and to crown it with His fullest blessing. Nothing could fit Abraham for this but a crowning act of obedience. When he had bound his son on the altar, God came and said to him, "By Myself

I have sworn . . . blessing I will bless you, and multiplying I will multiply your descendants as the stars of the heaven. . . . In your seed all the nations of the earth shall be blessed, because you have obeyed My voice" (Genesis 22:16–18).

To Isaac He said, "I will perform the oath which I swore to Abraham your father . . . because Abraham obeyed My voice" (Genesis 26:3, 5).

When will we learn how unspeakably pleasing obedience is in God's sight, and how immeasurable the reward He gives for it? The way to be a blessing to the world is to be people of obedience, known by God and the world by this one mark—a will completely yielded to God's will. Let all who profess to walk in Abraham's footsteps walk in this way.

Visit Moses at Sinai: God gave him a message for the people: "If you will indeed obey My voice and keep My covenant, then you shall be a special treasure to Me above all people" (Exodus 19:5). In the very nature of things it cannot be otherwise. God's will is His glory; only by obedience to His will is it possible to be His people.

Take the building of the sanctuary in which God was to dwell. In the last three chapters of Exodus, we have the expression nineteen times: "According to all that the Lord had commanded Moses, so he did." And then: "The glory of the Lord filled the tabernacle" (40:34).

Again, in Leviticus 8 and 9, we have the same

expression repeatedly with reference to the consecration of the priests and the tabernacle. And then: "The glory of the LORD appeared to all the people, and fire came out from before the LORD, and consumed the burnt offering" (9:23–24). Words cannot make it plainer. It is in that which the obedience of His people has produced that God delights to dwell, and He crowns the obedient with His favor and His presence.

After the forty years' wandering in the wilderness, and its terrible revelation of the fruit of disobedience, there was again a new beginning when the people were about to enter Canaan. Read Deuteronomy and all that Moses spoke when in sight of the land. You will find there is no book of the Bible that uses the word *obey* so frequently or speaks so much of the blessing obedience will certainly bring. The whole is summed up in the words "Behold, I set before you today a blessing and a curse: the blessing, if you obey the commandments of the LORD your God . . . and the curse, if you do not obey" (Deuteronomy 11:26–28).

". . .*the blessing, if you obey*. . ." is the keynote of the blessed life. Canaan, just like the Garden, and heaven itself, can only be a place of blessing if it is a place of obedience. Oh, that we would grasp it! Beware of praying only for a blessing. Let us seek first obedience, and God will supply the blessing. Our constant question as a Christian should be "How can I obey and please God perfectly?"

The next new beginning we have is in the appointment of kings in Israel. In the story of Saul, we have the most solemn warning as to the need of exact and entire obedience in the one whom God is to trust as ruler of His people. Saul had been commanded by Samuel to wait seven days for him to come and sacrifice and to show Saul what to do (1 Samuel 10:8). When Samuel delayed (13:8–14), Saul took it upon himself to sacrifice. When Samuel came, he said, "You have not kept the commandment of the LORD your God, which He commanded you. For now the LORD would have established your kingdom over Israel forever. But now your kingdom shall not continue. The LORD has sought for Himself a man after His own heart, and the LORD has commanded him to be commander over His people, because you have not kept what the LORD commanded you" (13:13–14). God will not honor the man who is not obedient.

Saul had a second opportunity to show what was in his heart. He was sent to execute God's judgment against Amalek. In this, he obeys. He gathers an army of two hundred thousand men, undertakes the journey into the wilderness, and destroys Amalek. But while God had commanded him to "utterly destroy all that they have, and do not spare them" (15:3), he spared the best of the cattle and King Agag. God speaks to Samuel, "I greatly regret that I have set up Saul as king, for he has turned back from following Me, and has not performed My commandments" (15:11). When Samuel comes, Saul says, "I have performed the commandment of the LORD" (15:13). And many would think he had. But his obedience was not complete. God claims exact and full obedience. God had told him to "utterly destroy all . . . and do not spare them." Saul had not done this. He had spared the best sheep for a sacrifice unto the Lord. And Samuel said, "To obey is better than sacrifice. . . . Because you have rejected the word of the LORD, He also has rejected you" (15:22–23).

It is a sad example of most obedience—which in part performs God's commandment, but still is not the full obedience God asks. God says of all sin and all disobedience: "Destroy it all! Spare not!" May God reveal to us whether we are indeed doing all He asks, seeking utterly to destroy all and spare nothing that is not in perfect harmony with His will. It is wholehearted obedience, down to the minutest details, that alone can satisfy God. Let nothing less satisfy you. Because while we say, "I have obeyed," God says, "You have rejected the Word of the Lord."

Just one word more from the Old Testament: Next to Deuteronomy, Jeremiah uses most the word *obey*. How sad to see that it is mostly in connection with the complaint that the people had not obeyed. God sums up all His dealings with the fathers in one thought: "For I did not speak to your fathers, or command them in the day that I brought them out of the land of Egypt, concerning burnt offerings or sacrifices. But this is what I commanded them, saying, 'Obey My voice, and I will be your God, and you shall be My people'" (Jeremiah 7:22–23). Oh, that we could learn: All that God speaks of sacrifices, even of the sacrifice of His beloved Son, is subordinate to the one thing: that all be restored to full obedience. Into all the inconceivable meaning of the words "I will be your God," there is no entrance but one: to obey His voice.

Now let us look at the New Testament. Here the prominence our blessed Lord gives to obedience comes to mind at once. Jesus, who entered it with His declaration "I come to do your will, O God," always confessed to men, "I seek not my own will, but the will of him who sent me." Of all He did and of all He suffered, even unto death, He said, "This commandment have I received of my Father."

If we turn to His teaching, we find throughout that the obedience He rendered is the same He requires of everyone who would be His disciple. During His whole ministry, from beginning to end, obedience was the very gateway to finding salvation. In the Sermon on the Mount He gives the admonition: "Not everyone who says to Me, 'Lord, Lord,' shall enter the kingdom of heaven, but he who does the will of My Father in heaven" (Matthew 7:21). And in His farewell discourse, how wonderfully He reveals the spiritual character of true obedience as it is born of love, is inspired by it, and as it opens the way into the love of God: "If you love Me, keep My commandments. And I will pray the Father, and He will give you another Helper, that He may abide with you forever. . . . He who has My commandments and keeps them, it is he who loves Me. And he who loves Me will be loved by My Father, and I will love him and manifest Myself to him. If anyone loves Me, he will keep My word; and My Father will love him, and We will come to him and make Our home with him" (John 14:15–16, 21, 23). No words could express more simply or more powerfully the inconceivably glorious value Christ puts on obedience, with its twofold possibility: Obedience is only possible to a loving heart, but it also makes possible all that God has to give us through His wonderful Holy Spirit, primarily His indwelling presence. I know of no passage in Scripture (John 14) that gives a higher revelation of the spiritual life or the power of loving obedience as its condition. Let us pray earnestly that the light of God's Holy Spirit may infuse our daily obedience with His glory.

See how all this is confirmed in the next chapter. How well we know the parable of the vine. How often and how earnestly we have asked how to abide continually in Christ. We have imagined that more study of the Word, more faith, more prayer, or more communion with God would surely be the keys, but we have overlooked a simple truth: "He who has my commandments and keeps them, it is he who loves Me." So again, obedience is the key. And "If anyone loves Me, he will keep My word; and My Father will love him, and We will come to him and make Our home with him." For Him as for us, the only way under heaven to abide in the divine love is to *keep the commandments.*

Obedience on earth is key to pleasing God's heart. Did you know that? Have you heard it preached? Have you believed it and proved it true in your experience? Unless there is some similarity between God's wholehearted love and our wholehearted loving obedience, Christ cannot manifest himself to us, God cannot abide in us, and we cannot abide in His love.

We find in the book of Acts two messages of Peter's that show how our Lord's teaching had become a part of him. (1) "We ought to obey God rather than men" (5:29). (2) "And we are His witnesses to these things, and so also is the Holy Spirit whom God has given to those who obey Him" (5:32). Full obedience is faithfulness unto death. Nothing on earth hinders the one who has given himself to God.

Paul singles out the phrase "obedience to the faith among all nations for His name" (Romans 1:5) as his motto for his service as an apostle. As Adam's disobedience, and ours, causes death, so the obedience of Christ, and ours, is the way of restoration to God and His favor.

James warns us not to be hearers of the Word only, but doers, and gives us an example in Abraham, who was justified by faith, but perfected by his works.

In Peter's first epistle, the first chapter, we see the place of obedience. In verse 2, he speaks to the "elect according to the foreknowledge of God the Father, in sanctification of the Spirit, for *obedience* and sprinkling of the blood of Jesus Christ" (emphasis added). This points to obedience as the eternal purpose of the Father, the great objective of the work of the Spirit, and a chief factor in the salvation of Christ. In verses 14 and 15 he writes, "As obedient children, not conforming yourselves to the former lusts, as in your ignorance; but as He who called you is holy, you also be holy in all your conduct." Obedience is the starting point of true holiness. In verse 22 we read, "Since you have purified your souls in obeying the truth . . ." The acceptance of the truth of God was not merely a matter of intellectual assent or emotional persuasion; rather, it was submission of the whole life to the supremacy of the truth of God. The Christian life was, in the first place, obedience.

John uses strong statements: "He who says, 'I know Him,' and does not keep His commandments, is a liar, and the truth is not in him" (1 John 2:4). Obedience is the hallmark of Christian character. He says, "And whatever we ask we receive from Him, because we keep His commandments and do those things that are pleasing in His sight" (3:22). Obedience is the secret of a good conscience and of the confidence that God hears us. The obedience that keeps His commandments becomes the outward expression of our love for God.

We may ask ourselves, "Does obedience take that place in my heart and life?" Have we given obedience the place of authority that God intends it to have: the motivation of our every action and our boldness to approach Him? If we yield ourselves to the searching of God's Spirit, we may find that we have not given implicit obedience the importance it deserves in our life, and that this is the cause of our failure in prayer and in our work. The deeper blessings of God's grace and the full enjoyment of God's love and nearness have been beyond our reach simply because obedience was never given the importance God gives it—the starting point and the goal of our Christian life.

May God awake in us an earnest desire to know His will fully concerning this truth. Let us ask the Holy Spirit to show us how far short we fall in our Christian life where obedience does not rule. May He help us see how that life can be exchanged for one of full surrender to absolute obedience to God's will in all things. As the disobedience of Adam in the Garden closed the gate, and the obedience of the Second Adam opened it, obedience in us opens the way for God to come and dwell in our hearts and be at home there.

May God make obedience—the one sacrifice He asks of us—the sacrifice we freely offer Him.

— Chapter 2 —

The Obedience of Christ

*For as by one man's disobedience many were
made sinners, so also by one Man's obedience
many will be made righteous.*

Romans 5:19

*Do you not know that to whom you present
yourselves slaves to obey, you are that one's slaves
whom you obey, whether of sin to death, or of
obedience to righteousness?*

Romans 6:16

"By one Man's obedience many will be made righteous." How much we owe to Christ! Though in Adam we were made sinners, in Christ we are made righteous. Here we see to what it is in Christ that we owe our righteousness. As Adam's disobedience made us prone to sin, the obedience of Christ makes possible our righteousness. To the obedience of Christ we owe everything. This is one of the richest among the treasures of our inheritance in Christ. How many have never studied this truth so as to love it and delight in it and receive the full blessing of it! May God, by His Holy Spirit, reveal its glory and make us partakers of its power.

Concerning the truth of justification by faith, Paul teaches in Romans 3:21–5:11 what its foundation was: the atonement of the blood of Christ. He shows its way and its condition: faith in the free grace of a God who justifies the ungodly. He tells of its fruit: the imparting of the righteousness of Christ, which gives immediate access to the favor of God and implants the hope of glory.

Then he unfolds the deeper truth of the union with Christ by faith, in which justification has its root, and which makes it right and possible for God to accept us for His sake. Going back to Adam and our union with him, with all its consequences, Paul proves how perfectly natural and reasonable it is that those who receive Christ by faith, and are thus united with Him, become partakers of His righteousness and of His life. Paul especially emphasizes the contrast between the disobedience of Adam with its condemnation and death and the obedience of Christ with the righteousness and the life it brings. As we study the place Christ's obedience took in His work for our salvation and see in it the very root of our redemption, we will know what place it should have in our heart and life.

Again, "By one Man's obedience many will be made righteous." How is this possible? There was a twofold connection between Adam and his descendants—the *judicial* and the *vital*. Through the judicial, the whole race, though yet unborn, came at once under the sentence of death. Death reigned from Adam to Moses, even over them—such as little children—that had not sinned in any manner like Adam's transgression. This judicial relationship was rooted in the vital connection. The sentence could not have come upon them if they had not been in Adam. Again, the vital became the manifestation of the judicial; each child of Adam enters life under the power of sin and death. "By one man's disobedience many were made sinners," both by position subject to the curse of sin and by nature subject to its power.

Adam is the type of Him who was to come—the Second Adam, the Second Father of the race. Adam's disobedience in its effect is the exact similitude of what the obedience of Christ becomes to us. When a sinner believes in Christ, he is united to Him and by a judicial sentence is at once pronounced and accepted as righteous in God's sight. Again, the judicial relationship is rooted in the vital. He has Christ's righteousness only by having Christ himself and being in Him. Before he knows much of what it means to be in Christ, he can know that he is acquitted and accepted. But he is then led on to know the vital connection and to understand that equally real and complete as was his participation in Adam's disobedience with the death and sinful nature that followed, so is his participation in Christ's obedience with the righteousness, obedient life, and nature that come from it.

The one thing God asked of Adam in the Garden was obedience. The one thing by which a creature can glorify God or enjoy His favor and blessing is obedience. The single cause of the power of sin in the world and the ruin it has caused is disobedience. From Adam we have inherited a tendency to willfulness, to selfishness, to disobedience. The whole curse of sin on us is due to Adam's disobedience, which we, of course, have also chosen. By our own choice we become "the children of disobedience." Clearly, the one work for which we needed Christ was to remove this disobedience—its curse, its dominion, its evil nature, and all its workings. Disobedience is the root of all sin and misery. The first objective of His salvation was to cut away the evil root and restore man to his original destiny—a life of obedience to God.

How did Christ do this? First, by coming as the Second Adam to undo what the first had done. Sin made us believe that it was humiliating to be always seeking to know and do God's will. Christ came to show us how noble, how blessed, how pleasing to God a life of obedience is. When God gave us the robe of creature-hood to wear, we did not know that its beauty, its unspotted purity, could only come from obedience to God. Christ came and put on that robe himself to show us how to wear it. Christ overcame disobedience and gives us the power to replace ours with His obedience. As universal and all-prevailing as was the disobedience of Adam, greater still was the power of the obedience of Christ.

The object of Christ's life of obedience was three-fold:

1. as our *example*, to show us what true obedience was;
2. as our *surety*, by His obedience to fulfill all righteousness for us;
3. as our *head*, to prepare a new and obedient nature to impart to us.

And so He died to show us that full obedience is a readiness to obey to the uttermost, even to die for God. Whatever the disobedience of Adam touched, it was to be renounced and replaced by the obedience of Christ. Judicially, by that obedience we are made righteous. Just as we were made sinners by Adam's disobedience, we are at once justified and delivered from the power of sin and death by Christ's sacrificial death. We stand before God as righteous people. We are made one with Christ in His death and resurrection so that we are as truly dead to sin and alive to God as Christ is. And the life we receive in Him is none other than a life of obedience.

To know what obedience is, consider how the obedience of Christ is the secret of our righteousness and our salvation. Obedience is the very essence of that righteousness. Obedience results in our salvation. His obedience, first of all to be accepted, trusted, and rejoiced in, as covering and making an end of my disobedience, is the one unchanging, never-to-be-forsaken ground of my acceptance. Then, just as Adam's disobedience was the power that ruled my life and was the power of death in me, Christ's obedience becomes the life-power of my new nature. I now understand why Paul in this passage so closely links righteousness and life: "Therefore, as through one man's offense judgment came to all men, resulting in condemnation, even so through one Man's righteous act the free gift came to all men, resulting in justification of life" (Romans 5:18). The more carefully we trace the parallel between the first and Second Adam, the more we see how in the former, death and disobedience reigned in his seed and how both were equally transmitted through union with him. By the same token, the more will the conviction be placed upon us that the obedience of Christ is equally to be ours not only by imputation but by personal possession. It is inseparable from Him that to receive Him and His life is to receive His obedience. When we receive the righteousness that God offers us freely, it points us to the obedience out of which it was born, with which it is inseparably one, and in which alone it can live and flourish.

This connection is discussed in the next chapter. After having spoken of our life-union to Christ, Paul, for the first time in the epistle (Romans 6:12–13), gives an injunction: "Therefore do not let sin reign in your mortal body, that you should obey it in its lusts. And do not present your members as instruments of unrighteousness to sin, but present yourselves to God as being alive from the dead, and your members as instruments of righteousness to God." Then he immediately proceeds to teach how this implies obedience: "Do you not know that to whom you present yourselves slaves to obey, you are that one's slaves whom you obey, whether of sin leading to death, or of obedience leading to righteousness?" Your relationship to obedience is a practical one; you have been delivered from disobedience (Adam's and your own), and now are become servants of obedience, and that "unto righteousness." Christ's obedience resulted in righteousness—the righteousness that is God's gift to you. Your submission to obedience is the way in which your relationship to God and to righteousness can be maintained. Christ's obedience leading to righteousness is the beginning of life for you; your obedience leading to righteousness is its continuance.

There is but one law for the head and the members. As surely as it was with Adam and his seed disobedience and death, it is with Christ and His seed obedience and life. The one bond of union, the one mark of likeness, between Adam and his seed was disobedience. *The one bond of union between Christ and His seed, the one mark of resemblance, is* obedience. It was obedience that made Christ the object of His Father's love (John 10:17–18) and our Redeemer. *Obedience alone* can lead us to dwell in that love (John 14:21, 23) and enjoy that redemption.

"By one Man's obedience many will be made righteous." Everything depends upon our knowledge of and participation in obedience as the gateway and the path to the full enjoyment of righteousness. At conversion, righteousness is given by faith once for all, completely and forever, even though there is little or no knowledge of obedience. But as this righteousness is embraced and submitted to and its full dominion over us as God's servants sought after, its nature will be revealed to us as born out of obedience and therefore ever leading us back to its divine origin. The truer our grasp of the righteousness of Christ in the power of the Spirit, the more intense will be our desire to share in the obedience out of which it sprang. In this light let us study the obedience of Christ so that we might live like Him as servants of obedience that results in righteousness.

In Christ this obedience is a life principle. The obedience of Jesus was not an act of obedience now and then, or even a series of acts, but the spirit of His whole life. He said in Hebrews 10:9, "Behold, I have come to do Your will, O God." He came into the world for one purpose: He lived only to carry out God's will. The one all-controlling power of His life was obedience. He wants to make it true in us, as well. This was what He promised when He said, "For whoever does the will of My Father in heaven is My brother and sister and mother" (Matthew 12:50). The link in a family is a common life shared by all and a family likeness. The bond between Christ and us is that He and we together do the will of God.

In Christ this obedience was a joy. "I delight to do Your will, O my God, and Your law *is* within my heart" (Psalm 40:8); "My food is to do the will of Him who sent Me, and to finish His work" (John 4:34). Our food is refreshment and vitality. The healthy man eats his bread with gladness. But food is more than enjoyment—it is a necessity of life. Doing the will of God was the food that He hungered after and without which He could not live, the one thing that satisfied His hunger, that refreshed and strengthened Him and made

Him glad. It was what David meant when he spoke of God's Word being "sweeter than honey and the honeycomb." As this is understood and accepted, obedience will become more natural, even necessary, to us; more refreshing even than our daily food.

In Christ this obedience led to waiting on God's will. God did not reveal all His will to Christ at once, but day by day, according to the circumstance of the hour. In His life of obedience there was growth and progress; the most difficult lesson came last. Each act of obedience fitted Him for the new discovery of the Father's next command. As obedience becomes the passion of our life, our ears will be opened by God's Spirit for His teaching, and we will be content with nothing less than divine guidance into the divine will for us.

In Christ this obedience led to death. When He said, "I do not seek My own will but the will of the Father who sent Me" (John 5:30), He was ready to go to any length in denying His own will and doing the Father's. He meant it. In nothing His will, at any cost God's will. This is the obedience to which He calls us and for which He empowers us. This wholehearted surrender to obedience in everything is the only true obedience, the only power that is able to carry us through. Oh, that Christians could understand that nothing less than this is what God rightly claims. Nothing less than this will bring the soul gladness and strength. As long as there is doubt about obedience and with it an underlying feeling of possible failure, we will lose the confidence that ensures victory.

But once we see that God requires total obedience—and promises help for it—we dare offer nothing less. We yield ourselves so His divine power can work, so His Holy Spirit can master our whole life.

In Christ this obedience sprang from the deepest humility. "Let this mind be in you which was also in Christ Jesus, who, being in the form of God, did not consider it robbery to be equal with God, but made Himself of no reputation, taking the form of a bondservant, and coming in the likeness of men" (Philippians 2:5–7). It is the one who is willing to be emptied, to become a servant, and is willing to be humbled before God and man to whom the obedience of Jesus will unfold its beauty and power. You may have a strong will that secretly trusts in self, that strives for obedience but fails. As we bow before God in humility, meekness, patience, and entire resignation to His will, and are willing to place ourselves in complete dependence upon Him, it will be revealed to us afresh that the blessing and responsibility of the creature is to obey God.

In Christ this obedience was by faith—in entire dependence upon God's strength. *I can do nothing of myself. The Father that dwells in me does the work.* The Son's unreserved surrender to the Father's will was met by the Father's unceasing and unreserved gift of His power working in the Son. And so it will be with us. If we learn that yielding our will to God is the measure of the power He gives us, we will see that surrender to full obedience is nothing but complete faith that God will work in us. The promises of the New Covenant rest on this: "I will give you a new heart and put a new spirit within you; I will take the heart of stone out of your flesh and give you a heart of flesh. I will put My Spirit within you and cause you to walk in My statutes, and you will keep My judgments and do them" (Ezekiel 36:26–27). Let us believe that God will work this in us, and we will have the courage to yield ourselves in unreserved obedience, even unto death. That surrender to God will lead to our conformity to God's Son, who did His Father's will, counting on His Father's power.

Do you know that being made righteous by Christ's obedience makes you like Him, and in Him you are servants of obedience that leads to righteousness? In the obedience of One the obedience of many has its root, life, and security. Turn and look upon, study, and believe in Christ as the obedient One. As His righteousness is our hope, let His obedience be our model for all of life.

Chapter 3

The Secret of True Obedience

*Though He was a Son, yet He learned obedience
by the things which He suffered.*

Hebrews 5:8

The secret of true obedience, I believe, is a clear and close personal relationship to God. All our attempts to achieve full obedience will fail until we have access to His abiding fellowship. *It is God's holy presence, consciously abiding with us, that keeps us from disobeying Him.* Imperfect obedience is the result of a life that is lacking. To defend our life by arguments and faulty motives will only make us feel the need of a more committed life, one that is entirely under the power of God, in which place obedience becomes natural. A life of broken and spasmodic fellowship with God must be healed to make way for a full and healthy life of obedience. The secret of true obedience, then, is the return to close and continual fellowship with God.

Christ learned obedience. And why was this necessary, you might ask. He needed to learn obedience so that as our great High Priest He might be made perfect. The Word explains that He learned obedience by the things that He suffered, and became the author of eternal salvation to all those who obey Him. Suffering is unnatural to us; it calls for the surrender of our will. Christ learned through suffering to give up His will to the Father at all costs. He became obedient unto death that He might become the author of our salvation. As with Him obedience was necessary to procure our salvation, so is obedience necessary for us to inherit it. Whether in His suffering on earth or in His glory in heaven, whether in himself or in us, the heart of Christ is set upon obedience.

On earth Christ was a learner in the school of obedience; from heaven He teaches it to His disciples on earth. In a world where disobedience reigns and results in death, the restoration of obedience is in Christ's hands. In His own life and in ours He has undertaken to maintain it. He teaches and works it in us. Think about what—and how—He teaches. How much have we yielded ourselves to be students in His school of obedience? When we think of an ordinary school, the principle elements are the teacher, the textbooks, and the students. Let us look at these in the context of Christ's school of obedience.

The Teacher

He *learned* obedience. And now that He teaches it, He does so first and primarily by unfolding the secret of His own obedience to the Father. I said that the power of true obedience is to be found in a clear personal relationship to God. It was so also with our Lord Jesus. Of all His teaching He said, "For I have not spoken on My own authority; but the Father who sent Me gave Me a command, what I should say and what I should speak. And I know that His command is everlasting life. Therefore, whatever I speak, just as the Father has told Me, so I speak" (John 12:49–50). This does not mean that in eternity Christ received God's commandment as part of the Father's commission to Him upon entering the world. No, day by day, each moment as He taught and worked, He lived, as man, in continual communication with the Father, and He received the Father's instructions as needed. Does He not say, "The Son can do nothing of Himself, but what He sees the Father do; for whatever He does, the Son also does in like manner. . . . For the Father judges no one, but has committed all judgment to the Son, that all should honor the Son just as they honor the Father. He who does not honor the Son does not honor the

Father who sent Him" (John 5:19, 22–23)? Even the words He spoke were not of himself, but of the Father that sent Him. Everywhere He revealed dependence upon a present fellowship and operation of God, hearing and seeing what God spoke and did and showed.

Our Lord always spoke of His relationship to the Father as the type and the promise of our relationship to Him and to the Father through Him. As it was with Him in relation to His Father on earth, so it is with us—the life of continual obedience is impossible without continual fellowship with the Son. Only when God comes into our lives to a degree and a power that many never consider possible, when His presence as the Eternal and Ever-present One is believed and received just as the Son believed and received it, can there be any hope of a life in which every thought is brought into captivity to the obedience of Christ.

The urgent need to receive our orders and instructions continually from God himself is implied in the words "Obey My voice, and I will be your God" (Jeremiah 7:23). The expression "obey the commandments" is seldom used in Scripture; it is rather "obey Me," or "obey, listen to *My voice.*"

With an army commander, a schoolteacher, or a father, it is not the code of laws and its rewards or threats—clear and good—that secures true obedience. It is the personal, living influence, awakening love and enthusiasm for the one who issues the instruction.

With us it is the joy of hearing the Father's voice that will fuel the joy and strength of true obedience in the hearer. It is the voice that gives power to obey the Word; the word without the living voice does not avail.

How clearly Israel illustrates this. The people heard the voice of God on Sinai and were afraid. They asked Moses that God not speak to them anymore. They wanted Moses to receive the Word of God and bring it to them. They only thought of the commands. They did not know that *the only power to obey* is in the presence of God and His voice speaking to us. And so with only Moses and the tablets of stone to speak to them, their whole history is one of disobedience, because they were afraid of direct contact with God. It is the same today. Many Christians find it so much easier to take their teaching from godly men than to wait upon God and receive it from Him. Their faith stands in the wisdom of men and not in the power of God.

Our Lord, who learned obedience by waiting every moment to see and hear the Father, has a great lesson to teach us: *It is only when, like Him, with Him, in and through Him, we continually walk with God and hear His voice that we can possibly attempt to offer God the obedience He asks.*

From the depths of His own life and experience, Christ teaches us this. Pray earnestly that God might show you the futility of attempting to obey without the same strength that Christ needed. Pray for a willingness to give up everything for the joy of the Father's presence.

The Textbook

Christ's direct communication with the Father did not take away His need of the Word. In the divine school of obedience there is only one textbook, whether for the adult or the child. In learning obedience, Christ used the same textbook as we have. And He appealed to the Word not only when He had to teach or to convince others; He needed it and He used it for His own spiritual life and guidance. From the beginning of His public life to its close, He lived by the Word of God. "It is written" was the sword of the Spirit with which He conquered Satan. The Spirit of the Lord God was upon Him; this word of Scripture was the consciousness with which He opened His preaching of the Gospel. That the Scriptures might be fulfilled was the light by which He accepted all suffering, even giving himself over to death. After the Resurrection, He expounded to the disciples from the Scriptures the things concerning himself. In Scripture He had found God's plan and path marked out for Him. He gave himself to fulfill it. In the use of God's Word, He received the Father's continual and direct teaching.

In God's school of obedience, the Bible is the only textbook. By this we know the disposition in which we are to come to the Bible—with the simple desire to find God's will concerning us, and to do it. Scripture was not written to increase our knowledge, but to guide our conduct, that as people of God we might be perfect, thoroughly furnished unto all good works. If anyone will do God's will, he shall know it. Learn from Christ to consider all there is in Scripture of the revelation of God. His love and His counsel are helps to God's great end: that God's people might be equipped to do His will as it is done in heaven, and to be restored to the perfect obedience upon which God's heart is set.

To appropriate the Word in His own life and conduct, to know when each particular portion was applicable, Christ needed and received divine teaching. It is He who speaks in Isaiah: "He awakens Me morning by morning, He awakens My ear to hear as the learned. The Lord God has opened My ear" (50:4–5). Even so does He who learned obedience teach us by giving us the Holy Spirit in our hearts as the Divine Interpreter of the Word. This is the great work of the indwelling Holy Spirit, to impress the Word we read and think upon into our heart and make it quick and powerful so that God's living Word may work effectively in our will, our mind, our whole being. When this is not understood, the Word has no power to effect obedience.

Let me be very plain about this. We rejoice in the increased attention given to Bible study and in testimonies about the interest awakened and benefits received. But let us not deceive ourselves. We may delight in studying the Bible, we may be enthused about the insights we get from God's truth; the ideas suggested may make a deep impression on us and awaken the most pleasing emotions, and yet the practical influence for making us holy or humble, loving, patient, and ready either for service or suffering may be very small. One reason for this is that we do not always receive the Word for what it truly is—the Word of the living God, who must himself speak it to us and into us if we are to know its full power. However we study or delight in the letter of the Word, it has no saving or sanctifying power without the Holy Spirit. Human wisdom and human will, however great their efforts, cannot command that power. The Holy Spirit is the power of God. It is only as the Holy Spirit teaches you as you read, only as the Gospel is preached in the power of the Holy Spirit, that you will be given, along with every command, the strength also to obey it.

With man, *knowing* and *willing, doing* and *performing* are different one from the other for lack of power, and sometimes even at odds. But *never is this so in the Holy Spirit*. He is at the same time the light and the might of God. All He is and does and gives contains the truth and power of God equally. When He shows you God's command, He always shows it to you as something possible to obey, as a divine gift prepared for you to do.

It is only when Christ, through the Holy Spirit, teaches you to understand and take the Word into your heart that He can really teach you how to obey as He did. Every time you open your Bible, believe that just as surely as you listen to the divine, Spirit-breathed Word, so will our Father, in answer to the prayer of faith and patient waiting, give the Holy Spirit's living operation in your heart. Let your Bible study be in faith. Do not merely believe the truths or promises you read—this may be in your own power—but *believe in the Holy Spirit; in His indwelling; in God's working in you through Him.* Receive the Word into your heart in the quiet faith that He will enable you to love it, yield to it, and keep it. Then our blessed Lord Jesus will make the Book to you what it was to Him when He spoke of the things written concerning Him. All Scripture will become the simple revelation of what God is going to do for you, in you, and through you.

The Student

Our Lord teaches us obedience by unfolding the secret of His learning it—in unceasing dependence on *the Father.* He teaches us to use the sacred Book, as He used it, as a divine revelation of what God has ordained for us, with *the Holy Spirit* expounding and enforcing it. If we consider the believer as a student in the school of obedience, we will better understand what Christ requires of us in order to do in us an effective work.

The attitude of a faithful student toward a trusted teacher is one of complete submission and perfect trust while giving as much time and attention as the teacher may require. When we acknowledge that Jesus Christ has a right to this kind of submission and trust, we can hope to experience how wonderfully He can teach us obedience like His own.

The true student of a great musician or artist yields his master wholehearted and unquestioning deference, as well. In practicing the scales or mixing colors, in the careful and patient study of the elements of his art, the student knows that it is wise to comply with and respect the one who has the greater experience and knowledge. It is this kind of surrender to His guidance and implicit yielding to His authority that Christ seeks. When we humbly ask Him to teach us how to obey God in everything, He asks us if we are ready to pay the price: it is to entirely and utterly deny self. It is to give up our will, our life, even unto death. It is to be ready to do whatever He says. The only way to learn to do a thing is to do it. The only way to learn obedience from Christ is to give up our own will and make the doing of His will the desire and delight of our heart. Unless we take the vow of absolute obedience as we enter this class in Christ's school, it will be impossible to make any real progress.

The true scholar of a great master finds it easy to

render him unwavering obedience because he trusts his teacher so implicitly. The student sacrifices his own wisdom to be guided by a higher wisdom. We need this confidence in our Lord Jesus. He came from heaven to learn obedience that He might teach it to us. His obedience is the treasury out of which not only the debt of our past disobedience is paid but also grace for our present obedience is given. In His divine power over our hearts and lives, He invites, He deserves, and He wins our trust and awakens in us a loving response. Just as we have trusted Him as our Savior to atone for our disobedience, let us trust Him as our teacher to lead us out of it and into a life of practical obedience. It is the presence of Christ with us throughout each day that will keep us on the path of true commitment to our task.

The path on which the Son himself learned obedience was long, and we must not wonder why it does not always come easily for us. Nor must we question if it sometimes requires more time at the Master's feet than most are ready to give. In Christ Jesus obedience has become our birthright. Let us cling to Him who learned the value of obedience and who by it gave us our salvation.

Chapter 4

The Importance of the Morning Watch in the Life of Obedience

For if the firstfruit is holy, the lump is also holy; and if the root is holy, so are the branches.

Romans 11:16

How wonderful and blessed is the divine appointment of the first day of the week as a holy day of rest. Not only to have one day of rest and spiritual refreshment amid the taxing busyness of life, but so that one holy day at the beginning of the week might sanctify the whole and equip us to carry God's holy presence into the week and its work to follow. If the firstfruit is holy, so is all the fruit; and if the root of the tree is holy, so are the branches. We are the branches.

There is gracious provision suggested by many

types and examples of the Old Testament by which an hour set aside at the beginning of each day enables us to assimilate a blessing for our work and gives us the assurance of victory over temptation. It is worth noting how in the morning hour the bond that unites us with God can be so firmly tied that during the hours when amid the rush of responsibility we can scarcely think of God, the soul can be kept safe and pure. It is true that the soul can so give itself away into His keeping in the time of private worship that temptation will serve only to draw us closer to Him. What cause for praise and joy that the morning watch can so renew and strengthen our surrender to Jesus and our faith in Him that the life of obedience can not only be maintained but also go from strength to strength.

In this chapter I want to consider the morning watch (or quiet time, whenever that is observed) in connection with the subject of obedience. The desire for a life of total obedience will give new meaning and value to the time spent alone with God, just as it can provide the motivation and persistence needed for this discipline.

Think first of the motivating principle that causes us to love and faithfully keep the morning watch. If we do it simply as our Christian duty, it will very soon become a burden. Or if our main purpose is our own happiness and safety, that alone will not supply the incentive to make such a time attractive. Only one thing will suffice to keep us faithful in communing with God—*a sincere desire for fellowship with Him.* We were created in God's likeness in the hope of spending eternity with Him. Fellowship with Him can equip us for a true and blessed life, both here and in the hereafter. To have more of God, to know Him better, to receive from Him the comfort of His love and strength, to have our life filled with His—for this He invites us to enter our closet and shut the door, so to speak.

It is in the place of quiet where we are alone with God that our spiritual life is both tested and strengthened. There is the battlefield where it is decided every day whether God will have all of us and whether our life will be one of absolute obedience. If we truly conquer there, committing ourselves into the hands of our Lord and finding a refuge in Him, the victory during the day is certain. It is there, in the inner chamber, where we prove whether we really delight in God and will make it our aim to love Him with our whole heart.

The first lesson is this: The *presence of God* is of supreme importance. To meet with God, to yield ourselves to His will, to know that we please Him, to have Him tell us His desires for the day and lay His hand upon us—this is what we can expect from our time of quiet and devotion. It is what we will come to long for and delight in.

Reading and meditating on God's Word is part of what occupies this hour. There are some points I would like to emphasize in this regard: one is that unless we are careful, the Word that should point us to God may actually hide Him from us. The mind may be interested, even delighted at what it finds, but because this can be merely food for thought, it may do us little spiritual good. If it does not ultimately lead us to wait upon God, to glorify Him, to receive His grace and power for sweetening and sanctifying our lives, it can become a hindrance rather than a help.

Another lesson that cannot be repeated too often, or pressed too urgently, is that it is only by the teaching of the Holy Spirit that we arrive at the true meaning of God's Word. Only by the Spirit will the Word penetrate our inner life and work in us. The Father in heaven, who gave us His Word with its divine mysteries and message, has given us His Holy Spirit within to interpret and appropriate that Word. The Father wants us to be taught by His Spirit. He wants us to enter into a teachable frame of mind and believe that the Spirit will make His Word live and work in us. We must remember that the Spirit is given to us that we should be led by Him, follow Him, have our whole life under His rule. He cannot teach us in the morning unless we give ourselves over to His leading. But if we do this and patiently wait on Him, not merely to receive new thoughts but to appropriate the power of the Word in our hearts, we can count upon His teaching. Let your closet be your classroom; let your morning watch be the study hour in which your entire dependence on and submission to the Holy Spirit's teaching is your aim.

Third, in confirmation of what we have already said: always study God's Word in the spirit of an unreserved surrender to obey. You know how often Christ and His apostles in their epistles speak of hearing and not doing. If you accustom yourself to studying the Bible without an earnest and definite purpose to obey, you will become hardened in disobedience. Never read God's Word concerning you without honestly yielding yourself to obey it at once and asking the grace to do so. God has given us His Word to tell us what He wants us to do and to show the grace He has provided to enable us to do it. How unfortunate when we think we are doing a good thing to read the Word without any conscious effort to obey it. May God keep us from this subtle sin. Let us make it a habit to say to God, *Lord, whatever I know to be your will, I will obey it at once.* Always read with a heart yielded in willing obedience.

Once again, I have referred to commands we already know and which are easily understood. But remember, there are a great many commands to which your attention may never have been directed, or others with so wide an application that you may not have grasped them. Read God's Word with a desire to know His will. If there are things that appear difficult, commands that look too steep, or for which you need divine guidance to know how to carry them out—and there will be those—let them serve to make you even more dependent on His help. It is not the text that is the easiest and most encouraging that brings the most blessing, but the text, whether easy or difficult, that throws you upon God. God would have us be filled with the knowledge of His will in all wisdom and spiritual understanding. This wonderful work is to be done in the quiet place. Remember, it is only when you know that *God is telling you to do a thing* that you can be sure He will give you the strength to do it. And only as we are willing to know all God's will does He reveal more of it to us.

What power the morning watch provides in the life of the one who makes a determined resolve to meet God there, to renew his surrender to absolute obedience, and to wait humbly and patiently on the Holy Spirit to be taught. If we can pray for ourselves, we can become an intercessor for others. In light of these thoughts, I will explain what prayer should include in the morning watch.

First and foremost, secure the presence of God. Do not be content with anything less than seeing the face of God, having the assurance that He is looking on you in love and listening to you. If our daily life is to be full of God, how much more the morning hour, when the day can have God's early blessing on it. In our Christian walk we want nothing so much as *more of God*—

His love, His will, His holiness, His Spirit living in us, His power working in us for others. There is no way of attaining this except by close personal communion. And there is no better time for securing and practicing it than in the morning. The superficiality of our Christian service comes from having so little real contact with God. If it is true that God alone is the source of love, goodness, and happiness, and that to have as much as possible of His presence, His fellowship, and His blessing is our highest joy, then surely to meet Him alone in the morning ought to be our aim. To have had God appear to them and speak to them was the secret of the strength of the Old Testament saints. Give God time alone so that He might reveal himself to you and your soul might call the place "Peniel"—for there you have beheld Him face to face.

After securing the presence of God, let the renewal of your surrender to absolute obedience for that day be a significant part of your morning sacrifice. Let confession of sin be clear—doing away with everything that grieves God. Pray for grace for a closer walk—asking and accepting it by faith. Let obedience to God be your determined resolve and controlling principle. There is no surer way—no other possible way—of knowing God's love and blessing in prayer than by aligning yourself with His will. This will avail more than your asking for anything. Let your prayer indeed be a "morning sacrifice," placing yourself as a whole burnt offering on the altar of the Lord. The measure of your surrender to full obedience will be the measure of your confidence toward God.

Remember that true prayer and fellowship with God cannot be one-sided. We must wait in His presence, waiting to hear His response. *This is the office of the Holy Spirit; He is the voice of God to us.* In the hidden depths of the heart, He can give certain assurance that we are heard, that we are well-pleasing, and that the Father will do for us what we have asked. To hear His voice and receive this assurance, we need the quiet stillness that waits on God, the quiet faith that trusts in God, the quiet heart that bows in humility before God and allows Him to be the answer to everything we ask. When we wait on God to take His part in our prayer, we renew our confidence that we will receive what we ask, that our surrender of ourselves in the sacrifice of obedience is accepted, and that we can count upon the Holy Spirit to guide us into all the will of God. What glory would come to us in the morning watch, and through it into our daily life, if the hour spent with God took conscious possession of us for the rest of the day. And how little need there would be to stir up a desire to keep that hour with our Savior.

And now for the last and best: In the life of our Lord Jesus, in His fellowship with the Father, the essential element was that it was all for others. This Spirit flows through every member of the body. The more we know it and yield to it, the more our life will be what God would have it.

The highest form of prayer is intercession. The chief object for which God chose Abraham and Israel and us was to make us a blessing to the world. We are a royal priesthood. As long as prayer is only a means of personal improvement and happiness, we cannot know its full power. Let intercession create in us a longing for the souls of those around us, a bearing of the burden of their sin and need, a pleading for the extension of God's kingdom, and labor in prayer for definite purposes to be realized. Let this kind of intercession be our concentration in the morning hour, and it will have new interest and attraction for us.

Oh, to realize what intercession means: to take the name and the righteousness and the worthiness of Christ, to put them on as a garment, and in them to appear before God! We are "in Christ's stead" to plead with God by name for individuals and their needs so that grace can do its work! With faith in our own acceptance before God, and the anointing of the Spirit to equip us for the work, we know that our prayer avails to "save a soul from death" and bring down the blessings of heaven to earth. It is inspiring to think that in the hour of the morning watch this work can be renewed and carried on day by day, each prayer closet maintaining its own communication with heaven, and helping together to bring down its share of the blessing. In intercession, more than in the zeal that works in its own strength, with little prayer, true Christlikeness is cultivated. Through intercession a believer rises to his true nobility in the power of imparting life and blessing, and it is through intercession that we will see an increase of the power of God in the church and its work among the lost.

In conclusion, think again about the intimate and vital connection between obedience and the morning watch. Without obedience there can be no spiritual power to enter into the knowledge of God's Word and His will. Without obedience there can be no confidence, boldness, or liberty to know we are heard. Obedience is fellowship with God in His will; without it there is no capacity for seeing and claiming and holding on to the blessings He has for us. So on the other side, without the living communion with God in the morning watch, the life of obedience cannot be maintained. There the vow of obedience can every morning be renewed in power and confirmed from above. There the presence and fellowship can be secured that makes obedience possible. It is there that by the obedience of the One, and our union with Him, strength is received for all that God asks. There the spiritual understanding of God's will is received that leads to a walk worthy of the Lord to all well-pleasing.

God has called us to live a life in the supernatural.

Allow your devotional time each day to be as the open gate of heaven through which light and power stream into your waiting heart, and from which you go out to walk with God all day.

— *Chapter 5* —

The Entrance Into a Life of Full Obedience

And being found in appearance as a man, He humbled Himself and became obedient to the point of death, even the death of the cross.

Philippians 2:8

Christ was obedient unto death. I will explain in this chapter about our entrance into a life of such obedience. You might think citing a text in which obedience is seen at its highest state of perfection is a mistake for our consideration of entrance onto this course. But it is no mistake. The secret of success in a race is to have the goal clearly defined and to have it as our aim from the outset. "[He] became obedient to the point of death." There is no other Christ for any of us, no other obedience that pleases God, no other example for us to copy, no other teacher from whom to learn obedience.

Christians suffer because they do not from the outset accept this as the only obedience for which they are to strive. Young people will sometimes find it a challenge to make nothing less than this their prayer and vow: *obedience unto death*. It is both the beauty and the glory of Christ to share in the highest blessing He has to give: the desire for and the surrender to it is possible even in the youngest believer.

A story in ancient history illustrates this obedience. A proud king, with a great army following him, demands submission from the king of a small but brave nation. When the ambassadors have delivered their message, the king of the small nation calls on one of his soldiers to inflict on himself a fatal stab wound. He does this at once, without question. A second is called; he too obeys the unusual command. A third is summoned; he too is obedient to death. Then the king tells the ambassadors, "Go and tell your master that I have three thousand such men. Let him come ahead, if he must." This king dared count upon men who didn't hold their life dear to themselves when the king's word called for it.

God desires such obedience of us. It is the obedience that Christ gave. It is the kind of obedience He teaches—let it be the same obedience and nothing less that we seek. From the very outset of the Christian life, let us avoid the fatal mistake of calling Christ Master but not doing what He says. Let all who are to any degree convicted of the sin of disobedience come and listen. God's Word will show the way to escape from such a life and gain access to the life Christ alone can give—a life of full obedience.

1. Confession and the Cleansing of Disobedience

In Jeremiah (the prophet who more than any other speaks of the disobedience of God's people), God says, "Go and proclaim these words toward the north, and say: 'Return, backsliding Israel,' says the LORD; 'I will not cause My anger to fall on you. For I am merciful,' says the LORD; 'I will not remain angry forever. Only acknowledge your iniquity, That you have transgressed against the LORD your God'" (3:12–13). Just as there can be no pardon at conversion without confession, neither can there be deliverance from the overcoming power of sin and disobedience after conversion without a new and deeper conviction and confession. Our disobedience must not be confessed in a vague generality; the specific things in which we actually disobey must be uncovered, confessed, abandoned, and given over to Christ to be cleansed away. Only then can there be hope of entering into the way of true obedience. Let us search our life in the light of our Lord's teaching.

Christ appeals to the law. He came not to destroy the law but to ensure its fulfillment. To the young ruler He said, "You know the commandments." Let the law be our first test. Take, for example, the sin of lying: I once had a note from a young lady saying that she wished to obey fully and that she felt compelled to confess an untruth she had told me. It was not a matter of great importance, and yet she rightly judged that the confession would help her to be cleansed. How much there is in society that will not stand the test of truthfulness.

There are other commandments also, up to the very last, that condemn all coveting and lusting after what is not ours, and in which too frequently the Christian yields to disobedience. All this must completely end; we must confess our disobedience and in God's strength put it away forever if there is to be any thought of our entering a life of full obedience.

Christ revealed the new law of love. To be as merciful as the Father in heaven, to forgive just as He does, to love our enemies and do good to them that hate us, and live lives of self-sacrifice and benevolence—this was the walk Jesus taught on earth. Let us consider an unforgiving spirit when we are provoked or taken advantage of, unloving thoughts and sharp or unkind words, the neglect to show mercy and do good and bless, as disobedience that must be felt, mourned over, and plucked out before the power of a full obedience can be ours.

Christ spoke much of self-denial. Self is the root of all our lack of love and obedience. Our Lord called His disciple to deny himself and to take up his cross; to forsake all; to hate and lose his own life; to humble himself and become the servant of all. He did so because self-will, self-pleasing, and self-seeking are the source of all sin. When we overindulge the flesh in such a simple thing as eating and drinking; when we gratify self by seeking or accepting what indulges our pride; when self-will is allowed to assert itself and we make provision for the fulfillment of its desire, we are guilty of disobedience to His commands. This clouds the soul and makes the full enjoyment of His light and peace impossible.

Christ claimed for God the love of the whole heart. For himself He equally claimed the sacrifice of all to come and follow Him. The Christian who has not in his heart made this his aim, who has not determined to seek for grace so to live, is guilty of disobedience. Much in his walk of faith may appear good and earnest, but he cannot possibly have the joyful consciousness of knowing that he is doing the will of his Lord and keeping His commandments if he has not surrendered his whole heart.

When the call is heard to come and begin anew a true life of obedience, there are many who desire to do so and try quietly to make a start. They think that by more prayer and Bible study they will grow into it—it will gradually come. They are greatly mistaken. The word God uses in Jeremiah might teach them their mistake: "Return, backsliding Israel," turn to Me. A soul that is in full earnest and has taken the vow of full obedience may grow out of a weak obedience into a fuller one. But there is no growing out of disobedience into obedience. A turning back, a turning away, a decision, a crisis is needed. And that comes only by a definite insight into what has been wrong and the confession of the same with remorse and repentance. Then alone will the soul seek for divine and mighty cleansing from all its filthiness, which prepares for the consciousness of the gift of a new heart, and God's Spirit in it, causing us to walk in His statutes. If you would hope to lead different lives, to possess a Christlike obedience unto death, begin by seeking God for the Holy Spirit of conviction to show you your disobedience and to lead you in humble confession to the cleansing God has provided. Rest not until you have received it.

2. Faith That Obedience Is Possible

This is the second step. To take it, we must understand clearly what obedience is.

First, we must look carefully at the difference between voluntary and involuntary sin. Obedience deals with the former alone. We know that the new heart that God gives His child is placed in the midst of flesh that has a sinful tendency. Out of this there often arise, even in one who is walking in true obedience, evil suggestions of pride, unloving or impure thoughts, over which he has no direct control. They are in their nature sinful, but they are not imputed as acts of transgression. That is, they are not acts of disobedience that one can prevent or cast out, as can be done with actions that are contrary to the law or God's will in which we have a conscious choice. The deliverance from them comes in another way—not through the will of the regenerate person, by which obedience comes, but through the cleansing power of the blood and the indwelling Christ. As the sinful nature rises, all one can do is to abhor it and trust in the blood that at once cleanses and keeps us clean.

It is extremely important to note the distinction. It keeps the Christian from thinking obedience impossible. It encourages him to seek obedience and practice it as a testimony to God's strength and enabling. In direct proportion to which the power of the will for obedience is utilized continually, so can the power of the Spirit be obtained and trusted to do the cleansing work in what is beyond the reach of the will.

When this difficulty has been removed, there is often a second one that arises to make us doubt whether obedience is possible. People connect it with the idea of *absolute perfection*. They put together all the commands of the Bible with all the graces these commands point to in their highest possible measure, and they imagine that a person with all these graces, manifested every moment to full perfection, is the only obedient servant. Of course, the demand of our Father in heaven is very different! He takes into account the various strengths and attainments of each of His children. He asks of us only the obedience of each day, or each hour at a time. He sees whether I have chosen to give myself to the wholehearted performance of every known command. He sees whether I am really longing and learning to know and do all His will. And when His child does this, in simple faith and love, the obedience is acceptable. The Spirit gives us the sweet assurance that we are well-pleasing to Him, and enables us to have confidence before God because we know that we keep His commandments and do the things that are pleasing in His sight. This obedience is an attainable degree of grace. The faith that it *is* attainable is indispensable to the obedient walk.

Do you ask for the ground of that faith in God's Word? It is found in God's New Covenant promise to write the laws on our hearts. And He puts a godly fear in our hearts so that we will not depart from Him. The greatest defect of the Old Covenant was that it demanded obedience but did not provide the power for it. The new heart delights in the law of God; it is willing and able to obey it. A promise of God is a thing of faith. If you do not believe it, you cannot appropriate it or put it to use.

To illustrate, imagine invisible ink on a paper. It

cannot be seen even if you witness the person writing on the paper. But if you are told what is being written, even though you still cannot see it, you accept by faith what is written. Hold it up to the sun or put a chemical on it, and the secret writing appears. It is as God's law written on your heart. If you believe it firmly and then submit your heart to the light of the Holy Spirit, you will find it true. To the one who desires to please God, the law written in the heart becomes the fervent love of God's commands *with the power to obey them.*

A story is told of one of Napoleon's soldiers. The doctor was seeking to extract a bullet that had lodged in the region of the heart, when the soldier cried, "Cut deeper; you will find Napoleon graven there." Is the law of God graven on your inmost being? Speak in faith the words of David and of Christ, "I delight to do Your will, O my God, and Your law is within my heart" (Psalm 40:8). The faith of this will assure you that obedience is possible; such faith will help you enter into the life of true obedience.

3. The Step From Disobedience to Obedience Through Surrender to Christ

"'Return, O backsliding children,'" says the LORD; 'for I am married to you. I will take you, one from a city and two from a family, and I will bring you to Zion. And I will give you shepherds according to My heart, who will feed you with knowledge and understanding'" (Jeremiah 3:14–15). They were His people, but had turned from Him; the return must be immediate and complete. To turn our back upon the divided life of disobedience, and in the faith of God's grace to say, "I will obey," may be the work of a moment.

The power for it, to take the vow and to maintain it, comes from the living Christ. We have said before, the power of obedience lies in the mighty influence of a living personal Presence. As long as we take our knowledge of God's will from a book or from men, we will only fail. If we take the ever-present Jesus as both our Lord and our strength, we can obey. The voice that commands is the voice that inspires. The eye that guides is the eye that encourages. Christ becomes all in all to us: the Master who commands, the Example who teaches, the Helper who empowers. Turn from your life of disobedience to Christ. Surrender yourself to Him in faith.

In surrender. Let Him have everything. Give up your life to be as full of His presence, His will, His service, as you know He wants it to be. Give yourself to Him not only to be saved from disobedience, or to be happy, but to live your life without deliberate sin and conflict. Yield so completely that He may have you wholly for himself as a vessel, as a channel, that He can fill with himself, His life, His love for the lost, and for use in His blessed service.

In faith. When a soul sees this new strength in Christ and the power for continual obedience, it needs a fresh faith to comprehend the blessing of His great redemption. The former faith understood the Atonement as Christ's obedience unto death. The new faith takes Scripture at face value and sees how Christ's obedience becomes ours: "Let this mind be in you which was also in Christ Jesus, who, being in the form of God, did not consider it robbery to be equal with God, but made Himself of no reputation, taking the form of a bondservant, and coming in the likeness of men. And being found in appearance as a man, He humbled Himself and became obedient to the point of death, even the death of the cross" (Philippians 2:5–8). It believes that Christ has put His own mind and Spirit into us, and in that faith, prepares to live and act as He did.

God sent Christ into the world to restore obedience to its rightful place in our hearts and lives, to restore man in general to obedience to God. Christ came, becoming obedient unto death, showing what the only true obedience is like. He lived it out and perfected it in himself as the life that He won through death and now communicates to us. The Christ who loves us, who leads and teaches and strengthens us, who lives in us, is the Christ who was obedient unto death. Obedience unto death is the essence of the life He imparts. Shall we not accept it and trust Him to perfect it in us?

Do you want to enter into the blessed life of obedience? See here the open gate: Christ says, "I am the Door." See here the new and living way: Christ says, "I am the Way." We begin to see that all our disobedience was because we did not know Christ. We see also that obedience is only possible in a life of unceasing fellowship with Him. The inspiration of His voice, the light of His eyes, the grasp of His hand, make it all possible.

Chapter 6

The Obedience Born of Faith

*By faith Abraham obeyed when he was called
to go out to the place which he would receive as
an inheritance. And he went out, not
knowing where he was going.*

Hebrews 11:8

Abraham believed there was a land of Canaan of which God had spoken. He believed in it as a "land of promise," guaranteed to him as an inheritance. He believed that God would bring him there, show it to him, and give it to him. In that faith he dared to go out, not knowing where he was going. In the blessed ignorance of faith he trusted God, and obeyed, and received the inheritance.

The land of promise that has been set before us is *the blessed life of obedience*. We have heard God's call to us to go out and to dwell there—about that there can be no mistake. We have heard the promise of Christ to bring us there and to give us possession of the land—that too is clear and sure. But do we desire that all our life and work be lifted to the level of a holy and joyful obedience? If so, our aim is high. It can only be reached by an inflow of the power of the Holy Spirit. By a faith that grasps a new vision and lays hold of the powers of the heavenlies, which are secured to us in Christ.

Let us review the themes we have been considering.

There is the *morning watch,* or the private devotional time. Our desire should be that we will be faithful to our keeping of this time and that it will be instrumental in growing our spiritual lives. We look to God to daily make it a time of intimate fellowship with Him, that it might involve a full surrender to His will in all things, lifting us into His presence and service for the entire day.

There is *Bible study.* We have seen that doing God's will is the only way to the full knowledge of God's truth. We have been challenged to read the Bible with the intention of obeying its commands.

There is the *spiritual help we are to give those around us,* watching over one another in tenderness, humility, and love, seeking the edification of others as much as our own.

There is *active service:* laboring for the lost not only at special seasons but at all times, in the patient perseverance of prayer and love. This is not a simple task. It is only possible when our sense of duty is inspired by the joy of His presence that accompanies our work for Him. Then there is the broader work—evangelism and missionary outreach.

As we contemplate cultivating in ourselves and others the conviction that we live only to please Him and to serve His purposes, some will say, "This is not a land of promise we are called to enter, but a life of burden and difficulty and certain failure." Do not agree with them! God calls us to a land of promise. Come and experience the honor of a Christlike obedience unto death. And see what blessing God will bestow on those who give themselves to the perfect will of God. Only believe in the glory of this good land of wholehearted obedience—in God, who calls you to it; in Christ, who brings you into it; in the Holy Spirit, who dwells in you and enables you to walk in it. He that truly believes enters in.

In speaking of our consecration, I will say that obedience is born of faith and that faith enables us to obey God. Five simple declarations are expressive of the disposition of a believing heart, the one who enters into the good land: *I see it, I desire it, I expect it, I accept it, and I trust Christ for it.*

1. Faith Sees It

In the previous chapters I have tried to show a "map of the land," to indicate the points at which God meets and blesses us. What we need to do by faith, quietly and firmly, is to settle the question: Is there truly a land of promise in which continuous obedience is possible? As long as there is any doubt on this point, it will not be possible to go up and possess the land.

Think about Abraham's faith. It rested in God, in His omnipotence and His faithfulness. I have put before you the promises of God. Here is another: "I will give you a new heart and put a new spirit within you; I will take the heart of stone out of your flesh and give you a heart of flesh. I will put My Spirit within you and cause you to walk in My statutes, and you will keep My judgments and do them" (Ezekiel 36:26–27). He adds, "I, the LORD, have spoken it and performed it" (Ezekiel 37:14). He undertakes to enable you to obey. Through Christ and the Holy Spirit He has made the most wonderful provision for fulfilling His plans and purposes in us.

If you do what Abraham did, you will fix your heart upon God. Abraham was strong in faith, giving glory to God, being fully persuaded that what He had promised He was able to perform. God's omnipotence was Abraham's anchor. Let it be yours. Look at all the promises God's Word gives of a clean heart, a heart blameless in holiness, of a life in righteousness, of a walk in all the commandments of the Lord, well-pleasing to Him, of God's working in us to will and to do of His good pleasure. In simple faith declare: *God says this; His power can do it.* Let this assurance possess you: a *life of full obedience is possible.* Faith can see the invisible and the impossible. Gaze on the vision until your heart says, *It must be true, it is true; there is a life promised that until now I have not known.*

2. Faith Desires It

When I read the gospel story and see how ready the sick and the blind and the needy were to believe Christ's Word, I ask myself what it was that made them so much more ready to believe than we are. The answer I find in the Word is this: one great difference lies in the honesty and intensity of their desire. They desired deliverance with their whole heart. There was no need to plead with them to accept His blessing.

And it should be no different with us! We wish in a halfhearted way to be better than we are. But how few there are who truly "hunger and thirst after righteousness"; how few who intensely long for a life of obedience and the continual consciousness of being pleasing to God. There can be no strong faith without strong desire. Desire is the great motivator in the universe. It was God's desire to save us that moved Him to send His Son. It is desire that moves people to study and work and sacrifice. It is a strong desire for salvation that brings a sinner to Christ. It is the desire for God and the closest possible fellowship with Him, the desire to be what He would have us to be and to have as much of His will as possible that will make the Promised Land attractive to us. It is this desire that will motivate us to forsake everything to gain our full share in the obedience of Christ.

How can the desire be awakened in us? How unfortunate that we need to ask the question, and that the most desirable of all things—likeness to God in union with His will—has so little attraction for us. It is a sign of our blindness and dullness, and I beseech God to give us by His Spirit enlightened eyes of the heart. Ask that you may see and know the riches of the glory of your inheritance awaiting your life of true obedience. Turn and gaze upon this life in the light of God's Spirit as truly attainable. Look again on it as inevitable, as divinely secured and divinely blessed, until your faith begins to burn with desire and say, "I do long to have it; with my whole heart I will seek it."

3. Faith Expects It

There is a great difference between desire and expectation. There is often a strong desire for salvation in a soul who has little expectation of obtaining it. It is a great step forward when desire becomes expectation, and the soul begins to say of spiritual blessing, "I am certain it is for me, and though I do not see how, I confidently expect to obtain it." The life of obedience is no longer an unattainable ideal held out before us that we might strive to get a bit closer, but it is a reality, meant for the here and now on earth. Anticipate it, expect it; God most certainly means for you to have it.

There is, of course, much to hinder this expectation: past failures, unfavorable temperament or circumstances, weak faith, apprehension as to what obedience unto death might demand, and a conscious lack of power for it. It all makes you say, "It may be for others, but I am afraid it is not for me." But to speak thus, you leave God out of your reasoning. Look to His power and His love and say, "Surely this life is for me!" Then expect it.

Take courage from the lives of God's saints who have gone before you. Saint Teresa [Teresa of Avila (1515–1582), Spanish Carmelite reformer, mystic, and writer] wrote that after her conversion, she "spent more than eighteen years in a miserable attempt to reconcile God and my life of sin." But at last she was able to write,

> I have made a vow never to offend God in the very least matter. I have vowed that I would rather die a thousand deaths than do anything of that kind, knowing I was doing it—this was obedience unto death. I am resolved never to leave anything whatever undone that I consider still to be more perfect, and more for the honor of my Lord.

She said further,

> We are so long and so slow in giving up our hearts to Thee. And then Thou wilt not permit our possession of Thee without our paying well for so precious a possession. There is nothing in all the world wherewith to buy the shedding abroad of Thy love in our hearts, but *our heart's love.* God never withholds himself from them who pay this price and persevere in seeking Him. He will, little by little, and now and then, strengthen and restore that soul, until it is at last victorious.

Gerhard Tersteegen [(1697–1769), German hymn-writer] had from his youth sought and served the Lord. After a time the sense of God's grace was withdrawn from him, and for five long years he was as one far away on the great sea, where neither sun nor stars appear: "But my hope was in Jesus." All at once a light broke on him that never went out, and he wrote, with blood drawn from his veins, a letter to the Lord Jesus in which he said,

> From this evening to all eternity, Thy will, not mine, be done. Command and rule and reign in me. I yield up myself without reserve, and I promise, with Thy help and power, rather to give up the last drop of my blood than knowingly or willingly be untrue or disobedient to Thee.

That was Tersteegen's obedience unto death.

Set your heart upon it and expect it. The same God lives today and works in His people. Set your hope on Him. He will not disappoint you.

4. Faith Accepts It

To accept is more than to expect. Many wait and hope and never possess because they do not accept God's gifts. To all who have not accepted, and feel as if they are not ready to accept, we say, *Expect*. If your expectation is from the heart and is set upon God himself, it will lead your soul to accept. To all who say they expect, we urgently say, *Accept*. Faith has the wondrous God-given power to say, "I accept it, I receive it, I have it."

It is because a definite faith is lacking to appropriate the spiritual blessings we desire that so many prayers appear to be fruitless. For such an act of faith not everyone is ready. In many cases, there is not a spiritual capacity to accept the blessing; it is where there is no true conviction of the sin of disobedience and consequently no true sorrow for it. Often there is not a strong longing or purpose to obey God completely in everything. In others, there is no deep interest in the message of Scripture: that God wants to perfect us to do His will, by His working in us that which is pleasing in His sight. In such cases the Christian is content to remain a babe. He wants only the milk of consolation. He is not mature enough to bear the strong meat of which Jesus ate: doing the will of His Father.

And yet we come to all with the entreaty "Accept the grace for this wonder-filled new life of obedience. Accept it now." Without it, one's act of consecration will come to naught. Any efforts to be more obedient will utterly fail. Has God not shown us that there is an entirely new position to take? It is an attainable position of simple childlike obedience day by day to every command He speaks through the Spirit. I ask you to take that position, to make that surrender, to accept that grace now. Enter into the true life of faith and consistent obedience. May your faith grow to be as unlimited and as sure as God's promises. Ask God to help you.

5. Faith Trusts Christ in Everything

All the promises of God are in Christ Jesus, and in Him they are sure and firm to the glory of God. It is possible that as you have considered the life of obedience, there have been questions and difficulties to which you cannot at once give an answer. Do you feel overwhelmed? Can you reconcile it with all your former habits of thought and speech and action? Are you afraid you will not be able immediately to subject everything to this supreme, all-controlling principle of obedience to all the will of God? To all these questions there is but one answer, one deliverance from all your fears: Jesus Christ, our living Savior, who knows everything and asks you to trust Him for the wisdom and the power to walk in the obedience of faith.

We have seen more than once how that His whole redemption is based on obedience—His and ours. He gives us the spirit of obedience—it is the spirit of our life. It comes to us each moment through Him. He takes charge of our obedience. He offers himself to us as guarantor for the maintenance of our obedience, and asks us to trust Him for it. In Jesus all our fears are removed, all our needs supplied, all our desires met. He, the righteous One, is your righteousness; He, the obedient One, is your obedience. Will you not trust Him for this? What faith sees and desires and expects and accepts, surely it will dare trust Christ to give.

Will you not today take the opportunity of giving glory to God by trusting Jesus to lead you into the Promised Land? Look up to your glorified Lord in heaven, and in His strength renew with new meaning your vow of allegiance, your vow never to do anything knowingly or willingly to offend Him. Trust Him for the faith to make the vow, for the heart to keep it, for the strength to carry it out. Trust Him, the loving One, by His living presence to secure both your faith and your obedience. Trust Him, and venture to join in an act of consecration, in the assurance that He undertakes to be its "Yea and Amen" to the glory of God.

Chapter 7

The School of Obedience

"Gather up the fragments that remain, so that nothing is lost."

John 6:12

In our study of obedience, there have been some points I did not have a chance to introduce and others I was unable to fully explain. I will speak about these now in an endeavor to help those in Christ's school of obedience.

1. Learning Obedience

First, let me warn against misunderstanding the expression "learning obedience." We are apt to think of absolute obedience as a principle, that obedience unto death is a thing that can only be gradually learned in

Christ's school. This is a great mistake. What we have to learn, and do learn gradually, is the *practice* of obedience, to new and ever more difficult commands. But as to the principle, Christ wants us from the very entrance into His school to vow complete obedience. A child of five can be as implicitly obedient as a youth of eighteen. The difference between the two lies not in the principle but in the nature of the work demanded. Though externally Christ's obedience unto death came at the end of His life, the spirit of His obedience was the same from the beginning. Wholehearted obedience is not the end but the beginning of our school life. The end is fitness for God's service, when obedience has placed us fully at God's disposal. A heart yielded to God in unreserved obedience is the one condition of progress in Christ's school and of growth in the spiritual knowledge of God's will.

Settle this matter once and for all. Remember God's rule: Give Him all and He will give you all. Consecration avails nothing unless it means presenting yourself as a living sacrifice to do nothing but the will of God.

2. Learning to Know God's Will

This unreserved surrender to obey is the first condition of entering Christ's school, and this alone equips us to receive instruction about the will of God for us. There is a general will of God for all His children, which we can, in some measure, learn from the Bible. But there is a special individual application of these commands—God's will concerning each of us personally—which only the Holy Spirit can teach. And He will teach it only to those who have taken the vow of obedience. This is the reason why there are so many unanswered prayers with regard to God making His will known. Jesus said, "If anyone wants to do His will, he shall know concerning the doctrine, whether it is from God" (John 7:17). If a man's will is truly set on doing God's will—if his heart is surrendered to do it and as a result he does it as far as he knows it—then he shall know what God has further to teach him. This is true of every scholar with the art he studies, of every apprentice with his trade, of every man in business—doing is the one condition of truly knowing. So in the spiritual realm, obedience—doing God's will as far as we know it and vowing to do all as He reveals it—equips us to receive the true knowledge of what God's will is for each of us.

In connection with this, three things are essential: (a) Seek a deep sense of your *ignorance of God's will* and of your impotence to know it by your own efforts. The consciousness of ignorance lies at the root of teachableness. "The meek will He guide in the way"—those who humbly confess their need of teaching. Head knowledge only gives human ideas without power. God by His Spirit gives a living knowledge that enters the heart and works effectually.

(b) Cultivate a strong faith that God *will make you to know* wisdom in the secret place of your heart. Perhaps you have known so little of this in your Christian life until now that the thought appears strange. Learn that God's working, and the place where He gives His life and light, is in the heart, deeper than all our thoughts. Any uncertainty about God's will makes joyful obedience impossible. Confidently believe that the Father is willing to make known what He wants you to do. Count upon Him for this. Expect it with certainty.

(c) Because of the darkness and deceitfulness of the flesh and the fleshly mind, ask God earnestly for *the searching and convincing light of the Holy Spirit.* There may be many things that you think acceptable but which your Father wants you to forsake. To consider it settled that these things are the will of God because you and others think so may keep you from knowing God's will for you in the matter. Without reservation, bring everything to the judgment of the Word, explained and applied by the Holy Spirit. Wait on God to lead you to know that everything you are and do is pleasing in His sight.

3. Obedience Unto Death

There is a deeper and more spiritual aspect of this truth. As a rule, it is something that does not come up in the earlier stages of the Christian life. And yet it is needful that every believer knows the privileges that await him as he progressively practices obedience. There is an experience into which wholehearted obedience will bring the believer, where he will know that as surely as with his Lord obedience leads to death.

What does this mean? During our Lord's life, His resistance to sin and the world was perfect and complete. Even so, His final deliverance from their temptation, His victory over their power, and His obedience were not complete until He had died to the earthly life and to sin. In that death He surrendered His life in complete relinquishment into the Father's hands, waiting to be raised up by Him. Through death He received the fullness of His new life and glory. And through death alone—the giving up of the life He had—could obedience lead Him into the glory of God.

The believer shares with Christ in this death to sin. In regeneration he is baptized into it by the Holy Spirit. Due to ignorance and unbelief he may know little experimentally of this complete death to sin. When the Holy Spirit reveals to him what he possesses in Christ, and he appropriates it in faith, the Spirit works in him the very same disposition that motivated Christ in His death. With Christ it was a complete ceasing from His own life, a helpless commitment of His spirit into the Father's hands. He completely fuifilled the Father's command: Lay down your life. Out of the perfect self-oblivion of the grave He entered into the glory of the Father.

Into this same fellowship the believer is brought. He finds that even in the most unreserved obedience for which God's Spirit equips him, there still remains a secret element of self and self-will. He longs to be delivered from it. In God's Word he is taught that this can only be through death. The Spirit helps him to claim more fully that He is indeed dead to sin in Christ and that the power of that death can work mightily in him. He is made willing to be obedient unto death, this total death to self, which makes him truly nothing. In this he finds a full entrance into the life of Christ. To see the need of this complete death to self and to be made willing for it, we must be led into the total self-emptying and humility of our Lord Jesus; this is the highest lesson in our school of obedience. This is indeed Christlike obedience unto death.

Space does not allow me to enlarge on this. In due time, God himself will teach this lesson to those who are entirely faithful.

4. The Voice of Conscience

With regard to the knowledge of God's will, we must give conscience its place and submit to its authority. In a thousand little things the law of nature or education teaches us what is right and good, but even earnest Christians do not always feel themselves bound to obey these. If you are unfaithful in that which is least, who will entrust you with greater things? Not God. If the voice of conscience tells you of a course of action that is nobler or better, and you choose something else because it is easier or pleasing to self, you ill-equip yourself for the teaching of the Spirit by disobeying the voice of God. A strong will to always do the right and to do the very best that conscience dictates is a will to do God's will. Paul writes, "I tell the truth in Christ, I am not lying, my conscience also bearing me witness in the Holy Spirit" (Romans 9:1). The Holy Spirit speaks through conscience. If you disobey and violate your conscience, you make it impossible for God to speak to you. Obedience to God's will is shown by a sensibility and respect for the voice of conscience. This is true with regard to eating and drinking, sleeping and resting, spending money and seeking pleasure. Let everything be brought into subjection to the will of God.

If you would live the life of true obedience, see that you maintain a good conscience before God and never knowingly indulge in anything that is contrary to His mind. Along with his love of God's Word, George Mueller attributed all his happiness during seventy years to the fact that he had maintained a good conscience in all things, not going on in a course he knew to be contrary to the will of God. Conscience is the guardian or monitor God has given you to warn when anything goes wrong. To the limits of the light you have, give heed to conscience. Ask God, by the teaching of His will, to give more light. Seek the witness of conscience as to whether you are obeying that light. Conscience will become your encouragement and your helper, and give you the confidence that your obedience is accepted and your prayer for ever-increasing knowledge of God's will is heard.

5. Legal and Evangelistic Obedience

Even when the vow of unreserved obedience has been taken, there may still be two sorts of obedience—that of the law and that of the gospel. Just as there are two Testaments, an Old and a New, so there are two styles or ways of serving God.

This is what Paul speaks of in Romans when he says, "For sin shall not have dominion over you, for you are not under law but under grace" (6:14), and further speaks of our being freed: "But now we have been delivered from the law, having died to what we were held by, so that we should serve in the newness of the Spirit and not in the oldness of the letter" (7:6). Again he reminds us, "For you did not receive the spirit of bondage again to fear, but you received the Spirit of adoption by whom we cry out, 'Abba, Father.'" (8:15). The threefold contrast points to a danger existing among Christians of still acting as if they were under the law, serving in the oldness of the letter and in the spirit of bondage. One great cause of the shallowness of so much Christian living is that it is more under the law than under grace. What is the difference?

What the law demands from us, grace promises and performs for us. The law deals with what we ought to do—whether we are able to or not—and by appealing to motives of fear and love stirs us to do our utmost. But the law gives no added strength, and so only leads to failure and condemnation. Grace points to what we cannot do, but offers to do it for us and in us. The law comes with commands on stone or in a book; grace comes in a living gracious Person, who gives us His presence and His power. The law promises life if we obey. Grace gives life, even the Holy Spirit, with the assurance that we can obey.

Human nature is always prone to slip back out of grace into the law, and secretly to trust in trying and doing its utmost. The promises of grace are divine; the gift of the Holy Spirit *to do all in us* is so wonderful that few believe it. This is the reason they never dare take the vow of obedience, or, having taken it, they turn back again. Study well what gospel obedience is. The Gospel is good tidings. Its obedience is part of that good tidings—*that grace, by the Holy Spirit, will do all in you.* Believe that. Obey in the joyful hope that comes from faith—a faith in the exceeding abundance of grace, in the mighty indwelling of the Holy Spirit, in the blessed love of Jesus, whose abiding presence makes obedience not only possible but certain.

6. The Obedience of Love

This is one of the special and most beautiful aspects of gospel obedience. The grace that promises to work all through the Holy Spirit is the gift of eternal love. The Lord Jesus (who takes charge of our obedience, teaches it, and by His presence secures it to us) is He who loved us unto death, who loves us with a love that passes knowledge. Nothing can receive or know love but a loving heart. This loving heart enables us to obey. Obedience is our loving response to the divine love resting on us, and is our only access to a fuller enjoyment of that love.

How our Lord insisted upon that in His farewell discourse! Three times He repeats it in John 14: "If you love Me, keep My commandments" (v. 15). "He who has My commandments and keeps them, it is he who loves Me. And he who loves Me will be loved by My Father, and I will love him and manifest Myself to him" (v. 21). "If anyone loves Me, he will keep My word" (v. 23). Is it not clear that love alone can produce the obedience Jesus asks and add the blessing that comes from obedience? The promise is that if we love Him and keep His Word, the Father and the Son will love us and make their abode with us—all these things are made possible to us through loving obedience.

In the next chapter He shows from the other side how obedience leads to the enjoyment of God's love. He kept His Father's commandments, and *abides in His love*. If we keep His commandments, we shall *abide in His love*. He proved His love by giving His life for us. We *are His friends*. We shall enjoy His love if we do what He commands us. Between His first love and our love in response to it, between our love and His fuller love in response to ours, *obedience is the one indispensable link*. True and full obedience is impossible, except as we live in love. This is the love of God, that we keep His commandments.

Beware of a legal obedience: striving after a life of true obedience under a sense of duty. Ask God to show you the "newness of life" that is needed for a new and full obedience. Claim the promise "The LORD your God will circumcise your heart and the heart of your descendants, to love the LORD your God with all your heart and with all your soul, that you may live" (Deuteronomy 30:6). Believe in the love of God and the grace of our Lord Jesus. Believe in the Spirit that is in you, enabling you to love, and so causing you to walk in God's statutes. In the strength of this faith, and in the assurance of sufficient grace, which is made perfect in weakness, enter into God's love and the life of living obedience it enables. *Nothing but the continual presence of Jesus in His love can prepare you for continual obedience.*

7. Is Obedience Possible?

This question lies at the very root of our life. The secret, half-unconscious thought that to live always well-pleasing to God is beyond our reach eats away at the very root of our strength. I strongly urge you to give a definite answer to the question.

Do you still fear that obedience is not possible— even in the light of God's provision for obedience, of His promise to work out His good pleasure in you and to give you a new heart with the indwelling of His Son and His Spirit? Then ask God to open your eyes to truly know His will.

If you are convinced in your mind and agree with this truth theoretically, but are still afraid to surrender yourself to such a life, ask God to open your eyes and to enable you to know *His will for you.*

Beware lest the secret fear of having to give up too much, of having to become too exclusive and entirely devoted to God, keep you back.

Beware of seeking just enough obedience to ease your conscience, and as a result to lose the desire to do and be and give God all He is worthy of.

Beware, above all, of "limiting" God, of making

Him a liar by refusing to believe what He has said He can and will do. If our study is to profit you at all, do not rest until you have truly learned that daily obedience to all that God wills for you is possible. In His strength yield yourself to Him for it.

But on one condition: not in the strength of your resolve or effort. Rather, yield to *the abiding presence of Christ and the continual teaching of the Spirit of all grace and power.* Christ, the obedient One, living in you, will ensure your full obedience. That obedience will be to you a life of love and joy in His fellowship.

— *Chapter 8* —

Obedience to the Last Command of Jesus

Go therefore and make disciples of all the nations, baptizing them in the name of the Father and of the Son and of the Holy Spirit.

Matthew 28:19

As You sent Me into the world, I also have sent them into the world. Peace to you! As the Father has sent Me, I also send you.

John 17:18; 20:21

These words breathe nothing less than the spirit of world conquest. "All the nations . . . all the world . . . every creature . . . the uttermost part of the earth"— each expression indicates that the heart of Christ was set on claiming His rightful dominion over the world He had redeemed and won for himself. And He counts on His disciples to undertake and carry out the work. As He stands at the foot of the throne, ready to ascend and reign, He tells them, "All authority has been given to Me in heaven and on earth" (Matthew 28:18) and points them at once to "the end of the earth" as the object of His and their desire and efforts. As the King on the throne, He himself will be their Helper: "I am with you always" (v. 20). They are to be the advance guard of His conquering hosts, even unto the end of the world. He himself will carry on the war. He seeks to inspire them with His own assurance of victory, with His own purpose of making this the only thing worth living or dying for—the winning back of all the world to God.

Christ does not teach or argue, ask or plead; He simply commands. He has trained His disciples in obedience. He has linked them to himself in a love that is able to obey. He has already breathed His own resurrection Spirit into them. He can count on them. He dares to say to them: "Go into all the world." Before, during His life on earth, they had more than once expressed their doubt about the possibility of fulfilling His commands. But here, as quietly and simply as He speaks these divine words, they accept them. No sooner has He ascended than they go to the appointed place to wait to be equipped by their Lord with heavenly power for heaven's work of making all the nations His disciples. They accepted the command and passed it on to those who through them believed on His name. Within a generation, simple men, whose names we do not even know, had preached the Gospel in Antioch and Rome and the regions beyond. The command was passed on and absorbed into the heart and life, as meant for all ages and for every disciple.

The command is for each one of us, too. There exists in the church of Christ no privileged clan to which alone belongs the honor, nor any servile clan on which alone rests the duty of carrying the Gospel to every creature. The life Christ imparts is His own life. The Spirit He breathes is His own Spirit. The one disposition He works is His own self-sacrificing love. By the very nature of His salvation, every member of His body, in full and vibrant access with Him, feels the desire to impart what he has received. The command is not an arbitrary law from without; it is simply the revelation that awaits our intelligent and voluntary consent of the full and wonderful truth. We are His body. We now occupy His place on earth. His will and love carry out through us the work He began, and now in His stead we live to seek the Father's glory in winning a lost world back to Him.

How miserably the church has failed in obeying the command! How many Christians there are who don't know that such a command even exists! How many hear of it but do not wholeheartedly try to obey it! How many seek to obey it, but only in the way and to the degree as seems fitting and convenient to them! We have professed to yield ourselves to wholehearted obedience. Surely we are prepared to listen gladly to anything that can help us understand and carry out our Lord's last and great command: *the Gospel to every creature.* What I have to say falls under three simple headings: *Accept His command, place yourself entirely at His disposal, and begin at once to live for His kingdom.*

1. Accept His Command

Various factors weaken the force of this command. There are the impressions that a command that is general in its nature, and given to all, is not as binding as one that is personal and specific; that if others do not do their part, our share of the blame is comparatively small; that where difficulties are very great, obedience cannot be absolutely demanded; and that if we are willing to do our best, this is all that can be asked of us. These attitudes are not obedience. This is not the spirit in which the first disciples obeyed. Surely this is not the spirit in which we wish to live with our beloved Lord. Why not resolve that even if no one else does, you by His grace will give yourself and your life to live for His kingdom? For just a moment forget everyone else and think of your own personal relationship to Jesus.

Are you a member of Christ's body? He expects every member to be at His disposal, to be animated by

His Spirit, to live for His purposes. It is so with our bodies. We carry every healthy member with us day by day in the assurance that we can count upon each to do its part. Our Lord has so truly made us a part of His body that He can ask and expect this same cooperation from us. And if we have truly yielded ourselves to Him, there can be no thought of our wanting anything except to know and to do His will.

Take the illustration of the vine and the branches in John 15. The branch, like the vine, has only one object for its existence—that of bearing fruit. If I really am a branch, I am—just as He was in the world—only to bring forth fruit, to live and labor for the salvation of men.

Take still another illustration: Christ has bought me with His blood. No slave apprehended by force or purchased with money was ever so entirely the property of his master as my soul, redeemed and won by Christ's blood, given over and bound to Him by love. My soul is His property, for Him alone to do with it what He pleases. He claims it by divine right, working through the Holy Spirit in infinite power, and I have given full assent to live wholly for His kingdom and service. This is my joy and my glory.

There was a time when it was different. There are two ways in which a man can bestow his wealth or service on another. Once long ago there was a slave who by his trade earned much money. All the money came to the master. The master was kind and treated the slave well. At length, from earnings his master had allowed the slave, he was able to purchase his liberty. In course of time the master became impoverished and had to come to his former slave for help. The slave was not only able but most willing to give it and gave liberally in gratitude for his master's former kindness.

You see at once the difference between the bringing of his earnings and service when he was a slave and his giving gifts when he was free. In the former case he gave all because both he and his money belonged to the master. In the latter he gave only what he chose to give. In which way ought we to give to Christ Jesus? I fear many give as if they were free to give whatever they choose—whatever they think they can afford. The believer for whom the purchase price of blood has acquired certain rights delights to know that he is the bondslave of redeeming love and to lay everything he has at his Master's feet because he belongs to Him.

Have you ever wondered how the disciples accepted the great command so easily and so heartily? They came fresh from Calvary, where they had seen the blood. They had met the risen One and He had breathed His Spirit into them. During the forty days, "through the Holy Spirit," He had given His commandments to them. To them Jesus was Savior, Master, Friend, and Lord. His Word had divine power; they could only obey. Let us bow at His feet and yield to the

Holy Spirit to reveal and assert His mighty claim. Let us unhesitatingly and with our whole heart accept the command and our life's sole purpose: the Gospel to every creature!

2. Place Yourself at His Disposal

The last great command has been so strongly linked with foreign missions that many are inclined to confine it to that realm of service exclusively. This is a great mistake. Our Lord's words "Go therefore and make disciples of all the nations, baptizing them in the name of the Father and of the Son and of the Holy Spirit" tell us what our aim should be. It is to be nothing less than to make every man a true disciple, living in holy obedience to all of Christ's will. And what a work there is to be done in our Christian churches and our so-called Christian communities before it can be said that the command has been carried out! How much the whole church and every believer in it need to realize that this work is the sole object of its existence! To bring the Gospel in a full, persevering, saving way to every creature is the mission and ought to be the passion of every redeemed soul. This alone is the Spirit and likeness and life of Christ formed in you.

If the church needs to preach one thing in the power of the Holy Spirit, it is the absolute and immediate duty of every child of God not only to take such part in this work as he may think fit or possible but to give himself to Christ the Master to be guided and used as He would have. And therefore, I say to every reader who has taken the vow of full obedience (dare we count ourselves true Christians if we have not?) to place yourself at once and wholly at Christ's disposal. As binding as is the first great command on all God's people, "You shall love the LORD your God with all your heart, with all your soul, and with all your strength," is the last great command, as well: "Go therefore and make disciples of all the nations, baptizing them in the name of the Father and of the Son and of the Holy Spirit, teaching them to observe all things that I have commanded you." Before you know what your work may be, before you feel any special desire or call or ability for any work—if you are willing to accept the command, place yourself at His disposal. As Master He will train and equip and guide and use you. Fear not; come now and forever away from the selfish religious practice that puts your own will and comfort first and gives Christ only what is left. Let the Master know that He can have you completely. Volunteer at once for His service.

The simple words "It is my purpose and desire, if God permit, to become a foreign missionary" have brought countless blessings into thousands of lives! It helped the individuals to surrender in obedience to the Great Commission, and it became a milestone in their lives. Only eternity will tell how many lives in those other lands were changed and blessed as the result of one person's obedience. Many who never can go abroad, or who think they cannot because they have not asked their Master's will, might be blessed if they would simply resolve by the grace of God to devote their life wholly to the service of Christ's kingdom. The external forsaking of home and friends and going abroad is often a great help to the volunteer in separating himself for Christ's work. The volunteer who works in his homeland may be able to continue in his calling and not need the external separation to keep him on track.

You who are students in the school of obedience, study the last and great commandment well. Accept it with your whole heart and place yourselves entirely at His disposal.

3. Begin at Once to Act on Your Obedience

In whatever circumstances you find yourself, it is your privilege to have within reach souls that can be won for God. And all around you there are numerous forms of Christian activity that invite your help and offer you theirs. Look upon yourself as redeemed by Christ for His service, as blessed with His Spirit to give you the very disposition that was in Him, and humbly but boldly take up your life calling of helping in the great work of winning back the world to God. Whether you are led of God to join some of the many agencies already at work or to walk in a more solitary path, remember not to regard the work as that of your church, or society, or even as your own—but as the Lord's. Cherish the consciousness of "doing it unto the Lord," of being a servant who is under orders and simply carrying them out. Then your work will not come between you and your fellowship with Christ, as it often does, but it will link you inseparably to Him, His strength, and His approval.

It is easy to become so engrossed in the human interest there is in our work that its spiritual character, the supernatural power needed for it, the direct working of God in us and through us—all that can fill us with true joy and hope—is crowded out. Keep your King on His throne. Before He gave the command and pointed His servants to the great field of the world, He first drew their eyes to himself on the throne. All power is given to Him in heaven and on earth. It is the vision, the faith of Christ on the throne, that reminds us of the need and assures us of the sufficiency of His divine power. Obey not a command but the living Lord of Glory. Faith in Him will give you heavenly strength.

Those words preceded the command to make disciples. And then there followed, "I am with you always." It is not only the glorious vision of Christ on the throne that we need, but Christ with us here below in His abiding presence, working for us and through us. Christ's power in heaven and His presence on earth—between these two pillars lies the gate through which the church enters for the conquest of the world. Let us follow our Leader, receive from Him our orders as to our share in the work, and never falter in the vow of obedience that has given itself to live wholly for His will and His work alone.

Such a beginning will be a training time, preparing us fully to know and follow His leading. If His call for the millions who are lost comes to us, let us be ready to go. If His providence does not permit our going, let our devotion at home be as complete and intense as if we had gone. Whether it is at home or abroad, if only the ranks of the obedient are filled up, Christ shall have His heart's desire, and His glorious commission—the Gospel to every creature—shall find its fulfillment!

Blessed Son of God! Here I am. By your grace, I give my life to the carrying out of your last great command. Let my heart be as your heart. Let my weakness be as your strength. In your name I take the vow of complete and lasting obedience. Amen.

More Classic Andrew Murray
Edited Especially for Today's Readers

Humility

In twelve brief but powerful chapters he takes readers on a journey through Scripture and Christ's life, showing us the utmost need for humility—as opposed to pride—in the Christian life. Demonstrating for us what Christ did when he took the form of a servant, Murray calls humility a distinguishing characteristic of the believer and encourages us to embrace this attitude in our own lives.

The Ministry of Intercessory Prayer

Murray offers practical, biblical instruction in intercessory prayer as well as a 31-day course, "Pray Without Ceasing," at the end of the book. All of this is part of his simple but profound goal to change the world through intercession.

Abiding in Christ

Using the image of the vine and the branches to explicate the concept of abiding in Christ, Murray offers a message as timely now as it was in 1895. He urges readers to yield themselves to Jesus in order to know "the full blessedness of abiding in Christ."

⬧BETHANYHOUSE